Visualizing Social Science

# Visualizing Social Science

PHOTOGRAPHS BY RACHEL TANUR

Social Science Research Council · New York · 2008

EDITOR Judith M. Tanur
DESIGNER Julie Fry
COLOR SEPARATIONS eddinsdesign, Providence, Rhode Island
PRINTER Meridian Printing, East Greenwich, Rhode Island
BINDERY Acme Bookbinding, Charlestown, Massachusetts


Typeset in Monotype Bembo & Corporate Expert
Printed on Finch Fine Bright White Smooth


Library of Congress Cataloging-in-Publication Data

Visualizing social science : photographs by Rachel Tanur /
editor Judith M. Tanur.
    p.   cm.
    Includes index.
    ISBN-13 978-0-9790772-4-1 (hardcover)
    ISBN-10 0-9790772-4-9 (hardcover)
    1. Social sciences—Pictorial works. 2. Manners and customs—
Pictorial works. I. Tanur, Rachel, 1958–2002. II. Tanur, Judith M.
III. Social Science Research Council (U.S.)
    H92.V57 2008
    300—dc22
                         2008004631

FOREWORD

ONE WAY IN WHICH WE CAN FRUITFULLY LOOK at what passed through Rachel's eyes is by using the thoughts of Anthony Giddens who informs us that one impact of modernity is that it poses a dilemma between "personalized and commodified" experiences. From this perspective we can conceive of the experience of travel away from the center of modernity as providing, on the one hand, personal escape from modernity via the belief that authentic, traditional, worlds still exist while, on the other hand, bringing us face to face with the modern reality of the juxtaposition of traditional and modern worlds. In the latter case objects from traditional worlds become commodities in the modern world. Rachel's photographs provide us with the opportunity to experience Giddens's point.

Rachel's images of traditional societies offer us the feeling of having gotten into a time machine to travel back in time. As such they provide us with some of the personal experiences that we strive for. We search for those personal, authentic, experiences precisely as a way in which to escape the routines, the lack of mystery, that legal-rational authority has generated in the modern world.

Who knows what is around the corner, but there right in front of the modern traveler is a scene so traditional that one is encouraged to accept the fact that there are new experiences to be had in life. Down there, down this street, is a world that feels unknown to the modern traveler. And that is precisely the appeal of the image. To be told about a traditional world is one thing, to be shown an image of it, of what we can be convinced it looks like, is to be offered the special gift of the opportunity to forget the modern.

Who has walked here and for how long have people done so? These images invite the viewer to go inward in order to construct a narrative. In the process of constructing a narrative the viewer is allowed to disengage from the contemporary world.

The image of a traditional work in progress by a fundamentally traditional-looking Guatemalan weaver (P. 26) allows the viewer to take in the beauty of the intense colors and the overall elegant harmony of the product itself.

When the traditional and the modern are juxtaposed, however, we are necessarily confounded by the way the modern intrudes upon the traditional and by the way what was once traditional takes on a commodified form even while holding onto the traditional look, for it is that indication of the traditional, the authentic, that is of value.

The large number of identical items of African pottery (P. 101) clearly indicates factory production. Nonetheless, the traditional pottery style speaks of individuality and authenticity. The commodification of traditional culture is evident here, but once these items are broken up and installed in the homes of individuals "back home," the air of the traditional is reestablished. Seeing tradition commodified is thus both artistically intriguing and socially revealing. The photograph of the Guatemalan tourist market (P. 21) is conceptually identical to that of the African pottery. Both provide us with insight into the commodification of traditional cultures.

Who will consume this modern presentation of traditional fruits on the Guatemalan fruit plate (P. 96)?

The image of Chinese men in a traditional market (P. 24) is reinforced by the two bundles of onions that sit before them. Deep into the image are other products and people on traditional bike haulers. The cropped image of the large blue truck with its load of produce indicates that the traditional and the modern are closer than mere attention to the men and their bundles of onions would indicate.

Rachel's photographs provide us with both conditions by which we can reach towards the authentic and the reality that we live in a global economy in which the authentic is commodified. As Giddens points out, it is attempting to manage those two realities that is a fundamental part of the modern human condition. Through her photographs Rachel has provided us with another opportunity to embrace the modern human condition.

*Richard Williams, Sociologist, Rutgers University*

Photographs and commentaries have been organized according to six thematic categories: WORK/COMMERCE (P. 10) *explores the role of individuals and markets in local economies;* TRANSPORT (P. 28) *compares modes of movement;* HOME (P. 38) *considers domestic environments and tasks;* LIFECOURSE (P. 56) *examines the youngest and most aged members of a society and the implications of the care of those people;* COSTUME/RITUAL (P. 72) *presents moments of celebration and contemplation; and* GLOBALIZATION (P. 90) *addresses issues raised by the fluidity between places and cultures.*

WORK/COMMERCE

THIS POWERFUL AND HIGHLY EVOCATIVE IMAGE, a child at work in adult dress wearing an adult expression, vividly captures the fate of millions of children in the third world. Forced into early labor, children are left with no choice but to sacrifice their childhoods, their freedom, their joy, their play, their true selves in order to survive.

But the sacrifice and employment of children is not just a developing world problem. Child abuse and neglect remain highly prominent in the first world. While we may not send our children to work in America and Europe, we have our own ways of stealing childhood from our children, of demanding that they sacrifice their needs to ours. While our children may not carry baskets on their heads, too many of our children, both rich and poor, carry inside them deep sorrow and crushing psychological burdens from parents who have been cruel, absent, ignorant, overwhelmed.

This beautiful photograph tells a profound and painful truth about children the world over, daring us to see.

*Daniel Levin, Ph.D., Clinical Psychologist, St. Louis*

WOMEN EVERYWHERE WORK TO SUPPORT THEIR FAMILIES. This is all the more visible in developing societies, for it is in such societies that women's work is absolutely central to the everyday well-being and survival of their families. As is true elsewhere, the types of work they do is sex-segregated. While men often range further from home, as fishermen, hunters, or migrants to distant cities, women's work is typically an extension of the home and their domestic responsibilities. They cook food, raise chickens, grow vegetables, or weave or sew garments to sell in local markets. In the markets, women can combine their family and work lives, selling their wares at the same time they are watching their children. Indeed, along with their mothers, children are often producers and sellers of the family's food and household wares, enlistees in the family's struggle to survive.

*Patricia A. Roos, Sociologist, Rutgers University*

THESE PHOTOS FIRST REMINDED ME of the colorful markets of my beloved city, Istanbul. Then I thought about the children in those markets; some behind the tables, trying to sell their goods. As a mother, I immediately felt that all the children should have been the buyers in those markets. After all, they were children. As a social scientist, however, I knew that this was just wishful thinking for the countries such as Turkey and Guatemala where child labor was still a fact of life.

Recent estimates on the participation rate of children in local markets show that Africa has the highest participation rate with 28%. It is 15% in Latin America and Asia, while it is below 1.5% in Europe. Research on this topic suggests that child labor is a direct result of poverty. Most parents in the developing world do not want their children to work, and studies show that the incidence of child labor decreases when family income increases. A large majority of the children who work in low-income countries are employed by their parents and work on the farms or in other family businesses. Even if some of them make an attempt to also go to school, these children generally have to sacrifice their education and hence face equally difficult futures. Researchers and policy advisers recommend that in addition to international legislation that protects children, policies that are aimed at increasing wealth and education in poorer countries would be the safest way to solve the child labor problem.

*Mihriye Mete, Political Scientist, Medstar Research Institute and*
*School of Advanced International Studies, Johns Hopkins University*


MARKETS ENRICH OUR LIVES by providing more opportunities than we would have in their absence. Economists have long studied their properties and benefits. Rachel's pictures remind us of the universality and diversity of markets and how they enrich us in ways other than by simply offering the opportunity (as the late nineteenth-century economist/sociologist Vilfredo Pareto noted) for "making someone better off without making someone else worse off."

*Paula Stephan, Economist, Andrew Young School of Policy Studies and NBER*

MARKETS ARE CROSSROADS, where strangers and friends connect, build ties, and find means of survival through the exchange of commodities and conviviality. A place where the chaos of movement and the seeming clutter of space give the impression of constant agitation. Yet all too frequently, business is slow and desperation settles in as vendors reflect on how they will feed their children or send them to school. Markets remind us that we are connected to the earth: pungent onions, fragrant spices, and ripe fruit are displayed carefully and beautifully to entice buyers. Market models and models of morality interpenetrate in a symphony of dissonance on the sidewalks of Greenwich village, the *suqs* of the Middle East, the *mercados* of Central and South America, the Tsukijii fish market of Japan, and the free markets of China. The sprawl of makeshift bricolage fascinates the tourist, irritates the keepers of order and modernity, and is irrepressible. Everything new and old is used in the market, ingenuity in the service of making ends meet. What is most remarkable about open-air markets is that, despite how mesmerizing and magical they seem to be in their disorderly variety, they tell more about the state and pulse of the world than newspapers, but only if one knows how to read them. They tell us who suffers and why. They speak to us of invasion and conquest, of debt and restitution, of dreams and death. As dusk arrives, coins are counted, a good sale remembered, and a little extra handed to a friend who has had a bad day. Exhaustion accompanies the symphony of rickshaws, tricycles, buses, trucks, rounded shoulders, hunched backs, and shuffling feet that head home. Some remain, sleeping in their stalls. For the time being, that may be all that exists of home.

*Linda J. Seligmann, Professor of Anthropology, George Mason University*


MUCH IS WRITTEN ABOUT THE SOCIAL CONSTRUCTION OF MARKETS and their embeddedness in the local social structures of relations. The photographs depict different Guatemalan markets in which Guatemalan women (and their children) sell the products of their own labor. These are women's markets: they reveal the social structure of the local community in which women complete the entire circle of production and sale of small-scale agricultural products and tourist goods. Men do not participate in these tasks. Do these markets reveal that men are away from home communities earning money in the cities or abroad, or have Guatemalan women traditionally sold their produce and crafts at the local markets?

*Ania Sher, Sociologist, Stony Brook University*

VILLAGE AND SMALL-SCALE INDUSTRIES produce important consumer goods and help to absorb surplus labor which in turn alleviates poverty and unemployment. They also ensure a more equitable distribution of national income, enhance balanced regional industrial development, act as a nursery for entrepreneurship, and facilitate the mobilization of local resources and skills which might otherwise remain unutilized. These striking photographs demonstrate the resolve and beauty of the entrepreneurial spirit that is found worldwide.

*Craig Coelen, Economist; Catherine Haggerty, Survey Methodologist; and*
*John Thompson, Statistician, National Opinion Research Center, University of Chicago*

OUTDOOR MARKETS, however colorful and vibrant, always project some degree of humility, especially when contrasted with our idea of a supermarket or when they are set against the background of imposing architectural structures.

And yet, the outdoor/street market scenes in Africa, China, Guatemala, and Europe become tools for capturing global inequalities. The presence (or absence) and the degree of rigidity of boundaries (between the products and the sellers; among the products, the sellers, and the environment; between the sellers and the potential customers; or among the different groups of sellers and products) are important factors in each scene as they become cues of different levels of economic development.

*Maria Vouyouka Sereti, Ph.D., Sociologist, Director of Educational Affairs,*
*Alexander S. Onassis Public Benefit Foundation (USA)*

FOOD IS A LUXURY. Having surplus to sell means you are not starving in a country where unemployment exceeds 50 percent in urban areas. Being able to buy or barter for food means you have the strength to do so in a country where as much as half of the adult population in some villages is HIV-positive. Going to the market means you have survived the ever-present danger posed by malaria. And the market captures the beauty of African women, their laughter and strength in the face of obstacles. Their elegance as they walk home carrying food on their heads and babies on their backs. Their determination and hope for a better life despite government policies and practices that often contribute to impeding their progress.

*Lynne Mitchnick, Sociologist, CEO, MR Solutions, Inc.,*
*Full-Service Global Market Research*

THE MEN AND WOMEN IN THESE PHOTOS represent a newly emerging social class in China: the rural-urban migrant workers.

From 1958 to 1978 the Chinese government prohibited farmers from leaving their countryside residences, and forced farmers to deliver their agricultural produce to the government at low prices so that the government could use income from the price differences between the industrial and agricultural products for industrialization, and to provide decent social welfare for urban residents. As a result, a rural-urban dual society emerged.

The most recent economic reform, which started in the 1980s, has gradually broken the rural-urban boundary. Rural residents have been allowed to find jobs in cities. However, in order to protect urban workers many local urban governments still have restrictions on what jobs the migrant workers can take. In addition, because migrant workers often have relatively low education and few skills, they have usually landed in the construction industry, the service sector, or factories, doing dirty, manual, and low-income work. They often face such problems as not being paid on time, extended working hours, poor living conditions, lack of health insurance, and separation from their children.

There were about 120–140 million rural-urban migrant workers in China as of 2005.

*Yingfeng Wu, Sociologist, New York Academy of Medicine*


THE PRESENCE OF A HUGE NUMBER OF PEASANT WORKERS IN CHINESE CITIES is a new and significant phenomenon following the economic reform in China after 1978. The large scale of rural-urban migration has first of all brought about a flourishing of the urban economy, mostly under public ownership. The small traders were the first ones to come to the cities and they were able to provide the urban residents with a convenient supply of fresh produce at free markets. Then there came to the cities people in almost all trades: housekeepers, small artisans, cooks and helpers, construction workers, contract workers, to name a few. Peasant workers were under a free labor market, a sharp contrast to the largely state-controlled labor system at the time, featuring lifetime employment and a low level of efficiency.

*Prof. Dr. Li Hanlin, Sociologist, Vice Director, Institute of Sociology,*
*The Chinese Academy of Social Sciences, Beijing, China*

AS PART OF MARKET REFORMS the Chinese government "decollectivized" agriculture, distributing land-use rights among village households. With a great deal more discretion over what they grow, peasants grow specialized crops for urban or semi-urban markets, often coordinating transportation to these markets.

*Eileen Otis, Sociologist, Stony Brook University*

CHINA'S POPULATION IS PROJECTED TO INCREASE from around 1.3 billion people in 2001 to about 1.5 billion in 2040. The proportion of those aged over 65 will increase from 7% of the population in 2000 to about 20% in 2040. Over the next forty years China will have to deal with several problems as a result of the increasing population (urbanization, sustainable agriculture, environment, health). China also faces the important problems associated with the increasing proportion of elderly people, which is mainly due to decreasing fertility, though also decreasing mortality. Furthermore, the very old, those aged over 80, will increase from about 8 million to about 50 million. Matching this, there will be a decrease in the ratio of working-age people to support each elderly person from 5 to 1 to 3 to 1. This essentially means that each working individual will be obliged to pay more to support the elderly as, to date, a market-oriented social security system has not succeeded in replacing the old all-encompassing state-run system. Of course, a market-oriented system will also face similar problems.

*Prof. Dr. Li Hanlin, Sociologist, Vice Director, Institute of Sociology,*
*The Chinese Academy of Social Sciences, Beijing, China*

THE PHOTOGRAPH OF A GUATEMALAN WOMAN WEAVING evokes an earlier, almost romantic, era of weaving and work—one which pre-dates that typically associated with the production of textiles: the cacophony of the industrial age with its clattering looms, cast-iron flywheels, and nimble fingers of artisans tying and retying broken threads among the thousands draped across the machinery. As the textile industry now fades from the American industrial scene with much of the nation's nondurable manufacturing base—and those work sites that remain being computerized spaces with power looms of air and water jets moving shuttles back and forth based on electronic design inputs—the legacy of this form of work and expression becomes increasingly invisible to us. This photograph confronts our modern understandings of manufacturing with a weaver using a simple backstrap loom (typically tied to a tree and wrapped around the individual for stability) with lee sticks (used to separate layers of fabric to keep patterns discernable during production)—a traditional form of craft production with designs usually passed from one generation to the next. Far from the more perfect textiles computerized looms produce today (which must meet a variety of industry codes and price-points to remain competitive), the patterns of cloth woven on a backstrap loom can be understood as representing the values and practices of everyday life within a community—with any "technical" mistakes a sign of authenticity in the work process and the worker's own individual charm. Just over the gentle sound of weft threads being passed with a wooden shuttle, this image whispers to us the meaning work can have in the life of an individual and community through the sheer beauty and power of weaving textiles.

*Patrick Moynihan, Sociologist, ABC News*
*Laura Johnson, Textile Designer, LGJ Design*

TRANSPORT

WITH THE CENTRALITY OF THE AUTOMOBILE TO EVERYDAY AMERICAN LIFE, it is easy to forget how peripheral—even insignificant—cars are to the majority of people on Earth. While in America there is about one car for every two people, in sub-Saharan Africa, there is about one car for every fifty people.

For most of the world, bicycles fill the central transportation mode that cars fill for America—there are 1.4 billion bicycles worldwide compared to 340 million automobiles.

These photos capture the utilitarian role bicycles play in many people's lives but also seem to depict the more personal relationship between bicycle and owner. These photos suggest a connection between bicycle and bicyclist. When the cyclist is present, as he is in the Cuban scene (P. 91), it is easy to imagine a bond much like the one that many Americans develop with their cars as the car/bicycle acts as symbol representing its owner's values and status.

*Martin Barron, Sociologist, National Opinion Research Center, University of Chicago*


THE PHOTOGRAPHS OF THE USE OF "ANIMATE" AS OPPOSED TO "MECHANICAL" power and energy are striking. Examples are the images of the French bicycle cart in "modern" France, a developed country; the African boatman (P. 29); the clothesline in Venice—again in "modern" Italy (P. 47); the Guatemalan communal laundry and clothesline images (PP. 42, 45); the Chinese man pulling a cart (P. 34); the Chinese woman carrying a pair of buckets (P. 23); the Guatemalan child carrying goods on her head (P. 11); and the Cuban man plowing (P. 33).

Persons living in the "developed"/industrialized world are so often caught up in Western/Eurocentric culture and technology that they take for granted that machines will take care of most of their tasks; they need to be reminded that so much of the world uses human or other animate sources of power to accomplish the tasks of everyday living.

Ms. Tanur's poignant images convey this message most strongly.

*David S. Gochman, Psychologist, Professor Emeritus, University of Louisville;*
*Director, Health Behavior Systems*

THESE TRADITIONAL PULL-CARTS are seen throughout urban China, carrying everything from vegetables to sell at the market, to furniture, appliances, and all manner of industrial supplies. One often sees such carts piled impossibly high with goods moving next to cars and traffic on the streets. They are pulled at a snail's pace by migrant workers who are populating China's urban centers and make their livelihood providing such services. Hence the pull-cart can be an important source of capital for migrant workers in cities.

*Eileen Otis, Sociologist, Stony Brook University*


IN STORES ALL OVER THE WORLD, we see items labeled "made in China." Yet compared with its large population, China's resources cannot even support its own people. One solution is "changing waste into treasure." Nothing is useless in China. Facing into the sun in the afternoon, a man is pulling a cart of collected waste, worth about 10–20 US dollars. He must be satisfied with the achievement today. There are two ways to collect waste. One is to wander around and pick it up, another is to buy it at a low price and sell it at a higher price. Most likely this man bought waste from residents. Usually, the buying price is half the selling price; 1 US dollar for 10 kg of newspaper or paper boxes, or 1 US dollar for 80 Coca-Cola cans, etc. There's a chain of markets for this. In the end the waste will be classified and sent to different factories to recycle.

*Guo Liang, Philosopher, Deputy Director, Center for Social Development,*
*The Chinese Academy of Social Sciences*


THIS MAN USES AN OLD-TECHNOLOGY CART to retrieve modern packaging. In China the means of transportation are changing from pulled carts to motorcycles. Soon people may see the pulled cart in a museum.

*Prof. Dr. Li Hanlin, Sociologist, Vice Director, Institute of Sociology,*
*The Chinese Academy of Social Sciences*

HOME

FOR ME, THESE PICTURES OF DWELLINGS IN DIFFERENT CULTURES are a reflection of the differences in income and standard of living of peoples across the world. Each house represents a summary of life in that part of the world. I remember being shown around a one-room house for many people, in a village in Zimbabwe. The Cuban street scene (P. 49) took me back to the poverty I saw in Cuba, Central America, Brazil, and elsewhere in Latin America. The Guatemalan houses (P. 50) reminded me of the variation in housing that people prefer, regardless of wealth. People are different, and like to remain so.

The colorful façade (P. 39) is fascinating. It is the essence of the combination of art and science. There is a science to arranging different squares of colors to make a pattern, but the art is found in the combination of the arrangement of colors and squares to be pleasing to the eye, and yet functional. It shows that the path between art and science often is blurred by a natural continuity that was understood by the photographer, Rachel Tanur, and one which pervaded and unified all of her architecture, her photography, and her legal work.

The African village, with the view of the variously shaped rooftops, reminds me of the explanation I was given of how a census was carried out in the South African homelands under apartheid. When I asked what method was used in South Africa to determine the population of a Black homeland I was told that they flew over the area, took pictures, and counted the number of roofs. This included the many roofs made out of a single section of corrugated aluminum. Then they estimated the maximum number of people who could possibly be living under such a roof, and multiplied the two figures.

*S. James Press, Statistician, University of California at Riverside*

LAUNDRY IS A NEAR-UNIVERSAL FACT OF LIFE. In our personal lives laundry is a burden. Each of us is troubled by it—haunted by it—in different ways. There is the dirty laundry that piles up needing to be done and the clean laundry that can sit for days waiting to be put away. Strangely, the loads of dirty clothes and the stacks of clean clothes relentlessly remind us of our inability to get control of this very basic aspect of our lives. We hide our laundry—both dirty and clean—like a dirty secret in the private spaces of our private homes. Yet, laundry is not always private, as these pictures remind us. Nor is it always dirty.

These photographs transform laundry into art. Isn't that the beauty of art, its ability to transform even the most mundane tasks into something somehow beautiful? In one picture, the laundry hangs, almost precariously, against the backdrop of forbidding, threatening clouds. In another, it hangs against a crumbling Italian wall (P. 47). And in a third it is being hand washed by women in the third world (P. 45). These photos remind us that laundry is the product of domestic labor. Although a near-universal fact of life, the form laundry takes and the way it hangs reflect the context in which it is done.

A theme that emerges from the laundry photos is technology, or lack thereof. Whether in Europe or Latin America, we see clean laundry that is hanging out to dry on someone's balcony or in her backyard. And in one photo, we see women meeting in a public place to wash the clothes and linens in the traditional way. All of this laundry has been cleaned in the absence of a washing machine, or at least in the absence of a dryer. The combined photos remind us of resource inequality between rich and poor. A washing machine is a labor- and time-saving device. A dryer works much faster to complete the task and takes much less time and effort to load than a clothesline. With a dryer, you don't have to cart a heavy basket full of soaking wet clothes outside, into the elements. You also don't have to stretch out each piece individually and reach up high to hang it carefully on the line. Those with access to a laundromat or to their own washer and dryer enjoy the convenience and time-saving aspects of these modern machines. At home, one can do laundry while multitasking. This is important to free up women, who in most societies are responsible for laundry, to pursue other activities, including paid work, housework, child care, or leisure. The possession of a washing machine and dryer is a symbol of social class in most cultures.

However, we also realize that, like other modern conveniences, household labor-saving devices aren't always panaceas. The industrial revolution promised that modern housework technology would fully free women from the burdens of this never-ending labor. But we now know that one of the unintended consequences of the technology is that society's standards of cleanliness adjusted to the available technology. People with washing machines wear their clothes fewer times before washing them, and social expectations are for clothes to have that "just washed" look and smell. Beds and towels get changed weekly and we tell ourselves that they ought to be for a healthy life. In a family of four with a washing machine and dryer, laundry can be a daily chore compared with once a week or less often if traditional methods are used. Further, just as with our gas-guzzling cars, modern laundry involves environmental social costs. Machine washing and drying consume more fresh water and much more of the world's precious power resources. They also release many chemicals into the environment. Nonetheless, it is likely that the people whose laundry hangs so picturesquely in the photographs would prefer to have a dryer in their home.

Possessing a clothes dryer is desirable and envied for more than its labor-saving attributes, however; the private aspect of indoor laundry is also important. The first thing we notice when we look at the photos of laundry hanging out is . . . the laundry hanging out, in public. It seems too obvious to mention, but people all over the world have their personal items hanging in public so that neighbors and passersby can see them and photos may be taken of them. In this sense, the photos invoke a certain voyeurism as we gaze at the personal items of strangers. Thus, one of the benefits of a dryer is the freedom to keep one's personal items, especially underwear, private and out of public view. Privacy of all sorts increases with income, including private spaces to sleep, bathe, and engage in leisure activities. Laundry, we are reminded, is another one of these sites.

Yet, while the laundry hanging in public may be seen as a negative, the photo of the women communally washing the laundry provides a reminder of something positive about traditional ways that the modern world has dismissed. While homemakers with washers and dryers suffer high rates of depression and social isolation from their individual, separate daily burdens, meeting others and working together lessens these feelings of anomie. Feeling part of a community is good for our psyches, if not our backs. Thus, the communal laundry transforms what could be private and isolating into a community-building activity that promotes social cohesion and a sense of belonging.

*Lisa Handler, Ph.D., Sociologist, Community College of Philadelphia*
*Julie E. Press, Ph.D., Sociologist, Independent Scholar*

WHY IS HANGING LAUNDRY OUTSIDE considered such a social taboo in the United States? It makes perfectly good sense if we're trying to save energy; it exposes stains to the most effective bleach there is (at least at certain times of the year, and especially in certain countries); it perfumes linens so they freshen a whole room for days; and almost every country I know cherishes the practice. Here the only industrialized country on view is Italy; but I have photos of laundry hung up to dry on balconies in Hamburg and Paris. Yet in the United States, the bylaws of every condominium and co-op forbid the practice; representatives of the neighborhood association come to call if the unwritten law is broken; and a homely practice with many benefits has fallen not only into disuse but into opprobrium.

How much oil could be saved, do you suppose, if laundry were dried outdoors when the weather permitted?

*Eleanor Singer, Sociologist, University of Michigan*


MANY PEOPLE, APPARENTLY, ARE TAKEN WITH PICTURES OF LAUNDRY ON THE LINE: silhouetted against the sky, contrasted with ancient stone or stucco walls. Rachel clearly was one of them; so am I. Part of what grabs us, I think, is aesthetic: the wonderful play of light on windswept cloth, the unconscious but still striking splash of colors, the very grounded local set against the very airy infinite, the very present in front of the very past.

There's also something social in our fascination: something about finding beauty in the mundane, something about finding meaning in the everyday-ness of laundry. There's nostalgia, of course: memories of our childhoods or longings for a past that we wish were better than we know it was. And family, of course: since the hanging of laundry is both a real and a symbolic act, signifying that someone is out there, caring for someone else.

But the person who did the work is absent. Would Rachel have taken those pictures if someone worn out from care giving, someone not very "picturesque" had been caught in the act of hanging that laundry? Would I like them less? Still want to hang them on my study wall?

*Ruth Schwartz Cowan, Historian, University of Pennsylvania*

THE BRILLIANT COLORS OF THE GUATEMALAN HOMES seem to represent the perpetual struggle of poverty-stricken people. The color is likely a light that inspires both hope and joy for local people. At the same time, it reflects their history and their own inner lightness despite the unending suffering of life in the developing world.

*Monique Centrone, Sociologist, Stony Brook University*

THE ROLE OF COLORS IN CULTURE is rather specific. On the one hand, people do not think much about colors in their everyday life. On the other hand, they pay great attention to them when choosing such goods as clothes and home furnishings. When a stranger visits an alien culture s/he understands that his/her color perception is rather different from the perception of those native to the culture. Natives pay attention to some colors and ignore others. Color perception becomes a part of tradition. These photos depict the variety of colors used by Guatemalans.

Putting these photos together we can notice that sets of colors used in decorating clothes, buses, and buildings are rather similar, with the palettes of colors being extremely varied. There are enormous gradations of red, blue, yellow on the clothes, the buildings, and to a lesser extent, the buses.

These photos illustrate a link between traditional culture and the globalization of cultures. We can see people in traditional clothes (PP. 2, 11, 13, 26), and a similar color spectrum decorates the buses (P. 36). Although vehicles are artifacts of modern civilization, the traditions of the Guatemalans transform them and they are assimilated in the structure of traditions. Buses decorated in this way, far from arousing discomfort in traditional people, become a part of their national culture thanks to this transformation.

*Nail Farkhatdinov, Sociologist, State University—Higher School of Economics, Moscow*

WHAT DOES IT MEAN to be a patriotic homeless person? The two flags are such a prominent part of this man's meager belongings. They are located in the front of the cart, placed higher than anything else he owns. Perhaps he even has a flag on his shirt; it is hard to tell. But what seems clear is that this man is proud to be an American.

Now I wonder, how does this photo make us, the viewers, feel? Does his pride shame us for our lack of patriotism? Does it make us want to do more for this man, to perhaps provide for him more tangible reasons for his pride? Or does it make us feel wonderment or skepticism that a person with so little could be so proud to live in this country?

Raising these questions now makes me question what the flag means to this man. Is it saying, "Don't screw with me," much like the Bush administration conveys to other countries? Is it a message to the terrorists? Does it signify that "Though homeless, I am one of you, I belong here"? Does it engender conversation from others? Or scare them away? Is he protecting against possibly harmful outside forces or trying to fit in with those around him?

Perhaps the flags are just colorful decorations he rescued from the trash.

*Carolyn Ellis, Sociologist, University of South Florida*

THIS HOMELESS MAN IN NEW YORK CITY pushes his possessions in a wagon that he topped with two American flags, symbols of the country that failed him. He appears to have on clean clothes and, indeed, his belongings include a bottle of laundry detergent. He may be homeless, but he does not give us the impression of hopelessness.

*Patricia Pugliani, Sociologist, Stony Brook University*

"AN ABSENCE OF POSITIVE SATISFACTIONS IN LIFE, rather than an increase in negative forces, is the main consequence of a depressive economic climate. It is the lack of joy in Mudville rather than the presence of sorrow that makes the difference." (N. M. Bradburn and D. Caplovitz, *Reports on Happiness*. Chicago: Aldine, 1965.)

*Norman Bradburn, Social Psychologist, National Opinion Research Center, University of Chicago*

THE PUBLIC WORK RELIEF PROGRAMS THAT THE DEPRESSION SPAWNED were said by some to have given men who were broke and broken new hope. Indeed, they caused a revival of hobo working culture that had developed from economic depressions at the end of the nineteenth century.

While working on urban construction or when on hiatus between rurally-based projects, the legions of this mobile and unattached workforce took up residence in the city center neighborhoods known as the Main Stem. Along with readily available single-room occupancy hotels (SROs) and employment agencies, the Stem had its bawdy houses, saloons, gambling enterprises, theaters, and all the sorts of things that enlivened the existence of the single working man.

Among the unintended consequences of supporting the hobo working force, however, was that men were wrested from normative lifecourse development and embodied a de facto counterculture. Post–World War II economic and social policy sought to eradicate the economic basis of hobemia so that the American Main Stems fell into disrepair, revealing a morally suspect and now literally bankrupt counterculture. Hobos who remained became known as bums, and the once vital economic center of the mobile workforce became skid row.

In the 1960s the *Social Science Encyclopedia* defined homeless specifically as dis-integration with the main normative (marriage and family) and the economic and political (work and civil society) institutions of society. Bums had lost all grasp on a legitimate position in civil society and were characterized as politically and morally impotent, homeless. They had not, by and large, lost their housing such as it was.

Scholars have tended to agree that contemporary American homelessness emerged between 1978 and 1982, the latter date defined by the success of activists in naming the new legions as homeless rather than tramps, hobos, bums, or bag ladies. The auspicious label, even if it was a political success, did nothing to tell us who these men, women, and children were, nor from where they came. A vast literature attempted to assign all manner of personal pathology to the victims of this massive social and economic development. A few analysts noticed a deep economic recession followed by an apparent recovery that did not touch the poorest ten percent of the population, the gentrification of skid row including demolishment of the nation's stock of SROs, and intra- and international job migration that left a new generation of the workforce suddenly without hope of employment.

When we studied them closely we found the homeless to be anything but dis-integrated. In fact, we found that they survived on little else than deep embeddedness in survival networks, and that these were often far more elaborate than the networks they could have called upon when they still did have housing. Could this be a nouveau-hobemia? What could be the long-term effects of engendering a counterculture consisting of citizens for whom we do not even provide housing?

Do not take this man's gaze lightly, for he may know better than you of a deep and brewing economic contradiction that may yet set asunder the foundations of the world's greatest economic force.

*J. Jeff McConnell, Sociologist, The J. David Gladstone Institutes,*
*University of California at San Francisco*

LIFECOURSE

IN THIS PICTURE OF AN ELDERLY AFRICAN WOMAN, Rachel captured a moment that challenges so many stereotypes of aging. This matured yet somewhat mischievous Maasai woman illustrates what we often forget.

Aging can be attractive. Her conspicuous face is framed with deep wrinkles around the narrow eyes, contrasting sharply with full lips not touched by time. Aging can be colorful and vibrant. She projects vigor and vitality despite a somewhat cynical look of perhaps one-too-many disappointments and unrealized dreams. Aging can be sensual. Her bald head is striking, reminiscent of the way in which bald heads of young women going through chemotherapy are sexy and sensual.

Rachel, being only in her 30s, used the camera to see far beyond her own frame of reference. With this picture she unveiled just slightly the mystery of the human pursuit of longevity and happiness.

*Wanda R. Lopuch, Administration and Supervision, Brain Fitness Institute*

RACHEL USED HER CAMERA to record the colors of difference. Like many travelers, she was a collector of people, costumes, streets, and landscapes that, when displayed in the United States, could only have been encountered on other shores. Looking at the color-drenched images, however, I am particularly struck by the fact that sometimes what is "exotic" is the unexpected appearance of familiar objects. For example, a Maasai woman displays her finery. A layered array of beautiful bead work, colorful necklaces, and what appears to be a set of house keys adorn the machine-made cotton of her dress and elaborate earrings emphasize her stretched earlobes and shaved head. In this photo, the local is constructed and framed by the juxtaposition of global elements—standardized items available across the globe.

*Naomi Rosenthal, Sociologist, SUNY College at Old Westbury*

I AM STRUCK BY THIS WOMAN'S DIRECT GAZE and crinkly, somewhat bemused smile; such a contrast to the Maasai women I first met in the Amboseli area in the early 1960s, when they would run in hiding if any men were with me. Even when I was alone or with my toddler, they would approach only after I had been, quietly but visibly, engaged in other things, in the area for a while. Often then, several giggly young women would approach, look around my vehicle, touch skin and hair and child but glance away from direct eye contact, soon depart to continue their trek to collect water, perhaps some firewood, and make the long journey back to their *manyatta* (temporary homestead) before dusk would bring elephants coming to water and more predators ready to hunt. This woman, perhaps in her forties, might be joined by her young daughters and granddaughters and her daughters-in-law, perhaps carrying their youngest children. Her daily routine has probably changed little over the decades, but her familiarity with *wazungu*, or strangers, is so evident in her comfortable, probing gaze and willingness to be photographed. How familiar was she with the photographer, we wonder? Does she still speak only *Maa* as her mother probably did, or does she share Swahili with some of those who are now around her? Does she have children who have gone to school? Surely grandchildren who are there now. Rather than carrying all her most special items against her body in a handmade leather bag that she would have throughout her adulthood, since she first married, she apparently leaves some behind in a locked box. Or does she now live in a permanent structure with a lock on the door? How much of her jewelry is recent, beads on wire, absent the cowry shells and beads sewed onto leather? Does she still make the more traditional pieces for special occasions or are these the new favorites? Is she a widow, as so many women are? A "co-widow" with a late husband's other wives? Is some young adult first son now starting a family and also responsible for his younger siblings, and is his mother having yet more children for which he will be responsible? Is her life better than her mother's and her grandmother's? Will her children's and grandchildren's world be one of even more arid land, fewer trees and less water, AIDS and malaria . . . and also schools, clinics, perhaps sources of income for women? I try to tell from her gaze but much is not known.

*Jeanne Altmann, Anthropologist, Princeton University*

A DAUGHTER LEARNS FROM HER MOTHER by following her footsteps, and sharing work, happiness, and sorrow along the way. The family is the most important institution in a society. It is impossible for a human being to become a member of a society without family experiences. Socialization begins at home. We learn by imitating our mothers, fathers, grandparents, siblings, and other significant others. A little girl experiences the outside world by chasing her mother's shadow. In developing countries, a little girl is expected to help her mother; she cleans, cooks, and raises smaller siblings.

*Hee-Choon Shin, Sociologist, National Opinion Research Center, University of Chicago*


ALL PHOTOGRAPHERS FACE A SET OF MORAL AND POLITICAL CHOICES about how to use their cameras and how to represent the people they depict. No camera is a passive tool, simply recording some external reality; cameras have the point of view of their owners. Is the camera a weapon, reducing the powerful to mere mortality (like Richard Avedon) or making the familiar strange and grotesque (like Diane Arbus)?

Rachel makes a choice to go the other way, in the tradition more of Dorothea Lange or Eve Arnold, reminding us of the simple dignity and even breathtaking beauty of the people over whom the economic machine runs in the march towards profits. Her photographs of Maasai women or Guatemalan peasants reveal a resilience and grace that is poetic in its simple beauty.

There is a marked gender difference in the photographs. The women relate to the camera, smile or stare directly into it, proud, tall, and engaged. The men seem far sadder; they look away from the camera, down, to the side, refusing to engage with the lens. Perhaps the toll is greater on them, since the penetration of the global market into traditional life not only displaces them from their land but also upends their traditional domestic privileges. The women may hold up half the sky, but they also seem to have their feet more firmly planted on the ground.

*Michael Kimmel, Sociologist, Stony Brook University*

MEMORY — WHETHER PERSONAL OR SOCIAL — is a tricky entity that is elusive, cunning, tempting, and full of magic. Memory promises a bridge to the past, to the way we were, to the way things were. And yet, this promise can never be fulfilled. If the past weren't a past, it would be here, with us. And of course, it is not. And the memory is an imperfect and unstable representation of the past. Whenever one attempts to touch the past — even with a smile — one is doomed to discover that there is no way one can touch what is gone. These are perhaps the hardest moments. Traveling to one's childhood home is a trying experience: the home that we remembered as huge, glorious, and warm seems later in life to be small, ugly, rundown, and estranged. The way to school which was long, full of temptations, is now short, and lacking any excitement. And those who went to school with us and whom we meet twenty years later are less witnesses of the past than witnesses of the present, of our aging, of the time that passes, and of the past that can never be re-enacted and relived. And the memory — through its picture of a rainy day and a shared umbrella and an optimistic smile and a sense of friendship — is perhaps our last defense against the recognition that the past is untouchable, that there is no way back, and that the loss is a loss.

*Vered Vinitzky-Seroussi, Sociologist, Hebrew University of Jerusalem*


THE CHINESE GOVERNMENT successfully implemented the one-child per family policy in urban centers, creating the conditions for the phenomenon known as "the little Emperor." With only one child for two sets of grandparents to dote on, the children born within the plan receive seemingly endless gifts and attention, prompting some to worry about a generation of spoiled children. Interestingly, many urbanites increasingly accept having a daughter as the only child. Whereas in rural China the family planning policy has led to the abandonment of daughters, in urban China the policy has led to an increased value placed on daughters, now the sole child in many families. Families invest in their daughters' education and future. It will be interesting to see how their families react in the future when these daughters confront the labor market discrimination against women that is widespread.

*Eileen Otis, Sociologist, Stony Brook University*

A WISE MAN ONCE SAID THAT A NATION IS AN IMAGINED COMMUNITY. Its boundaries are imagined through media, symbols, and collective memories of wars. One may wonder how these children imagine their nation. When will they realize the pictures of cute cartoons on their backpacks are from a country that once invaded their nation? When they realize it, will they despise these cartoons as part of a collective national memory or embrace them as part of their childhood memory? If every nation is imagined through the minds of innocent children, nationalism may not be a reason for conflict.

*Hwa-Ji Shin, Sociologist, University of San Francisco*

THE CHINESE WAY is for children to follow behind each other, rather than to hold hands in pairs as is done in the United States.

*Prof. Dr. Li Hanlin, Sociologist, Vice Director, Institute of Sociology,*
*The Chinese Academy of Social Sciences, Beijing, China*

IN 1970, PREMIER ZHOU ENLAI INITIATED the first involuntary population control campaign in the People's Republic of China (PRC). This campaign, which limited each Chinese couple to two children, was replaced in 1978 by more stringent family planning legislation. Commonly referred to as the one-child policy, this new legislation restricted most Chinese couples to one child.

In the late 1970s, Chinese officials and demographers alike were careful about the language that they used to describe the PRC's new population control efforts. With little reference to the fact that China comprised 20% of the world's population on 7% of the world's arable land, they stressed how fertility limits would hasten the modernization of China's national agriculture, industry, science and technology, and national defense.

As Vanessa L. Fong describes in *Only Hope: Coming of Age under China's One-Child Policy* (2004), this legislation has radically transformed the life of the average Chinese child. Like those captured in this photograph, these children have quickly become the center of the modern Chinese family unit and the PRC's burgeoning economy. Given an increase in the familiar and national resources now available to them, an extraordinary number of Chinese children can compete in a capitalist world system that they—and their nation—are helping to transform.

*Amy Traver, Sociologist, Stony Brook University*

IN NOVEMBER 2005, the nation's 50,000th Chinese adoptee joined an American family. Most of these families cherish a photograph just like this one; an image that captures the newly adopted child, with members of his or her orphanage cohort, in the lobby of the White Swan Hotel in Guangzhou, China.

Asian children have long comprised the majority in American inter-country adoption (ICA). In fact, many attribute the birth of ICA in America to the adoption of Japanese children after World War II. While over 100,000 Korean children have been adopted by parents in the United States since the end of the Korean War in 1958, China has recently emerged as the foremost "sending" Asian nation—and foremost "sending" nation, more generally—in American ICA.

Growing alongside this contingent of American families is public and academic interest in ICA from China. Cable news programs like National Geographic follow American parents' China adoption trips. US-based corporations like American Express and Kodak utilize China adoption storylines in their commercials. Newspaper articles with titles such as "Love has no borders: Couple bridges desire for children with Chinese adoptions" profile American families created through adoption. Additionally, as the headline "Love has no borders" also indicates, China adoption has also become a fertile case study for an expanding sociological literature on boundaries; it brings to life many of our most salient borders while it highlights their very permeability.

*Amy Traver, Sociologist, Stony Brook University*

MORE THAN A FIFTH OF THE WORLD'S POPULATION lives in China today. Even though the Chinese government has implemented a fairly strict one-child policy, the Chinese population will continue to grow until it is estimated to level off sometime before 2100. The policy was enforced with reward and punishment; it has been largely successful. This policy, however, is creating serious social issues such as gender imbalance (especially at marriageable ages) and orphans. The policy is somewhat controversial in terms of birth control methods, in particular, mass sterilizations and forced abortions.

*Prof. Dr. Li Hanlin, Sociologist, Vice Director, Institute of Sociology,*
*The Chinese Academy of Social Sciences, Beijing, China*

HE IS SKINNY, with only a worn cloth around his waist, sitting on a simple bench under a tree and surrounded by basic open-fire cooking equipment. By the standards of our "advanced society" we could dismiss him as merely a poor old man. Yet this old man projects anything but poverty or unhappiness. The lean, bent body still reveals muscular strength that hints at a great strength of will. His strong grip unusually contrasts with a white beard and balding head, illustrating that he embodies a great sense of vitality and perseverance. Most of all, the man's genuinely content smile expresses his inner happiness with who he is and how he lives.

Through her lens, Rachel underlines that happiness does not necessarily come from the comfort of material goods. All of these symbols are missing. Instead, we are overwhelmed with the warmth and happiness of basic human habitat.

Looking at this picture, one cannot escape questions about the nature and "achievements" of what we consider to be an advanced society.

*Wanda R. Lopuch, Administration and Supervision, Brain Fitness Institute*


AN AGING POPULATION is presenting a challenge globally. Most societies, especially the poorest ones, find it difficult to set aside scarce resources to take care of the elderly. It is estimated that US spending on the elderly will consume half of the federal budget by 2015; the United States is in far better shape than most of the developed world. The burden of an impoverished elderly class with a thin or nonexistent safety net will be especially acute. The Maasai woman (P. 57) seems to be reflecting on the lessons and experiences of what appears to have been a long and fruitful life.

*Craig Coelen, Economist; Catherine Haggerty, Survey Methodologist; and*
*John Thompson, Statistician, National Opinion Research Center, University of Chicago*

CULTURES THAT REVERE ELDERS are sustained by family systems and family lives that integrate the old and the young, and in which elders contribute productive work, family services, and valued knowledge of sacred or secular ways.

*Nancy Mathiowetz, Survey Methodologist, University of Wisconsin, Milwaukee*


COMMON AMONG ALL SOCIETIES is the fact that widely diverse family structures produce happy, healthy children. Children always benefit from the emotional nurturing and developmental support provided by caring adults, both men and women. Increasingly, societies are looking beyond fathers' economic responsibility to consider the other forms of support that fathers can and do give. Here a father and son in traditional African attire represent timeless family values in an increasingly modern Africa.

*Craig Coelen, Economist; Catherine Haggerty, Survey Methodologist; and*
*John Thompson, Statistician, National Opinion Research Center, University of Chicago*

COSTUME/RITUAL

CARNIVAL IS CELEBRATED THROUGHOUT THE WESTERN WORLD; it is particularly famous in New Orleans. What immediately comes to mind is the stark contrast between the white-faced images of the Venice festival captured here, and the pictures of those stranded in New Orleans in the wake of Hurricane Katrina, most of whom were African American. Indeed, when I think of New Orleans' most famous event, I think of whiteness; of white faces partially hidden by masks and masks painted white. Who would ever imagine in examining Mardi Gras, in its organization, in its media representation, in its exclusivity, in its old-line krewes, that New Orleans is 70% African American? Understanding the dynamics driving the way that Mardi Gras is constructed may very well provide a map for interpreting the posthurricane images that continue to haunt us.

*Beth Mintz, Sociologist, University of Vermont*


CARNIVAL TRADITIONS, usually associated with Catholicism, are found in Western Europe from Italy to Belgium; carnival also exists in West Africa (Senegal, Gambia, Guiné Bissau) where it is often independent of Christianity. Both African and European traditions fed the New World, where the creole cultures of the Caribbean islands and of New Orleans gave birth to the best-known manifestations of carnival. Venetian Carnevale is the archetypal expression of carnival in its European Catholic form. Rachel Tanur's photographs of the celebration in Venice offer a refreshingly personal, even idiosyncratic, view of carnival in the Lagoon. Composition and color, as in the marvelous photograph of cone-headed revelers (P. 79), move us out of the everyday world. Things are aslant, not quite representative of a comfortable normality. The camera here captures the magic of a transformative masquerade.

*Peter Mark, Art Historian, Wesleyan University*

THIS IS, FOR ME, AN ESPECIALLY EVOCATIVE PICTURE. Aesthetically, the composition is a pure delight, from the jaunty angles of the revelers' "cones," to the attitudes of their bodies in relation to each other. The colors of their costumes are also so bright and vibrant against the somber gray of the Venice backdrop. But that backdrop—and specifically the contrast between the "be here now" gaiety of the revelers and the intimations of decay and mortality that are everywhere in Venice—adds depth and an elegiac feel to the image. Knowing of the all-too-early death of the photographer invites a final parallel. In the photo's contrast between the "in the moment" vitality of the revelers and the impermanence of Venice, we see reflected the full arch of Rachel Tanur's short but exceptional life.

Finally, at the most general level, the image reminds us of what might be termed the "existential functions of the social." Whatever else social attachments do for us, they serve at a very basic level to hold our worst existential fears at arm's length. As Durkheim reminds us, life is never more meaningful than during periods of intense social engagement. Absorbed in the planning, anticipation, and actual events of Carnevale, the revelers temporarily banish their fears of aloneness, meaninglessness, and mortality . . . even as the somber backdrop of Venice reminds us of their inevitable presence in our lives.

*Doug McAdam, Sociologist, Stanford University*

WHAT IS STRIKING ABOUT THIS PICTURE is the way it brings the public and performative nature of prayer, a religious ritual, to the fore. Prayer, a ritual we tend to think of as so very private and internal, is revealed for its formalism and community-oriented nature. Further, it is interesting that this photo contains a subject in military uniform, which heightens the formalism. At the same time, the sweetness of the child in the center lightens and balances the darkness of the adults' garb. Additionally, the focus of the child, along with her light clothing, is easily seen as a purity and innocence of purpose, perhaps in contrast to that of the adults, whose collective attention is scattered and more vague, rendering them less than perfect in their spiritual endeavor.

*Monique Centrone, Sociologist, Stony Brook University*

CHINA DOES NOT HAVE REAL RELIGION, according to the Western standard. People could go to a Taoist temple to "worship" soon after they worshiped in a Buddhist temple. What they pray for are not spiritual but practical things, such as giving birth to a boy instead of a girl, or to have a good business. Standing at the center of the Temple of Heaven, where the emperors used to pray for good harvests, the five adults and the little girl are tourists. They are not serious, they are not displaying religiosity, they just wish to take photos.

*Guo Liang, Philosopher, Deputy Director, Center for Social Development,*
*The Chinese Academy of Social Sciences*

THE POWER OF THE STATE to regulate all aspects of human life—even contact with the Divine. Women pray, and a small child participates, for now. Corralled onto a small space, flanked by a soldier and a father or brother, are they protected or quarantined by patriarchal state power? Are they dissidents or a family of prayerful tourists?

*Donna Gaines, Sociologist, www.donnagaines.com*

THE PHOTO CAPTURES SOCIAL CHANGE in a very important aspect—the beliefs of Chinese after the economic reforms. Following the Marxist tradition, the Communists in China are generally atheists and consider religion as spiritual opium. During the extremist era of the Cultural Revolution (1966–1976), all religions were banned, and praying was declared as superstition and thus was banned as well. Since the 1980s, however, some people, especially women and/or the younger generation, have started to be interested in religious beliefs again. Praying in temples, which are also usually tourist places, has become a fashionable way of expressing good wishes. However, it is still not acceptable for many people, especially for the Communist cadres and military service personnel, because they are the backbone of the Communist regime. The photo clearly shows the different attitudes of members of the same family towards praying. The older man appears to be a Communist Party or government cadre, and the younger man is in the military. While their other family members are sincerely praying, they find it difficult to do so.

*Yingfeng Wu, Sociologist, New York Academy of Medicine*

ONLY WHEN WESTERNERS STAY IN CHINA can they understand why China has to conduct the "one family, one child" policy. There are too many people in China! Yet simply imagining the structure of one child as the focus of two parents and four grandparents suggests that there must be something wrong. Nevertheless, these "little emperors" are enjoying their happy lives right now, no matter what the future will be.

*Guo Liang, Philosopher, Deputy Director, Center for Social Development,*
*The Chinese Academy of Social Sciences*

RACHEL'S PHOTOS REFLECT HER RECEPTIVITY to such a broad variety of experience that they immediately raise questions about how to describe the relation of people, so apparently different, to one another, to other species, and to the environment, in this era of rapidly increasing communication and consequent globalization. Very importantly, many of the photos also portray these relationships layered in time.

Can the social sciences offer any unified or comprehensive theory of life adaptation that can help people live peacefully and productively in a world of such pronounced differences and inequities of wealth and condition?

These are the challenges that these photos raise for the social sciences. We need social science to help us understand the universals and the social and cultural resources that people bring to the task of bridging these differences.

In my own work in child development, one of the most heuristic frameworks for guiding the investigation of such questions as children's adaptation under stressful life conditions has been ecological theory, which focuses attention on the increasingly comprehensive layers of social and environmental context in which each individual is embedded. Within this framework, scientists can organize and conceptualize the study of the transactions that take place, both cross-sectionally and longitudinally, between the individual and the contextual layers that change the characteristics of both the individual and the contexts within which the individual functions.

*Suzanne Salzinger, Ph.D., Psychologist, Child and Adolescent Psychiatry, New York State Psychiatric Institute and Columbia University*

KITCH OR IRONY FREE? Faith peddled on a billboard. Come inside, have free coffee, counseling, prayer, and miracles. Set against a storefront window selling "stuff" we may wonder, is God just another commodity form, or why not? Why shouldn't comfort stations offer soul-weary travelers something hospitable for the Spirit?

*Donna Gaines, Sociologist, www.donnagaines.com*


RELIGION IN THE UNITED STATES is a dynamic social phenomenon. It shapes American society and is shaped by it in return in ways that are unique and surprising; ways that defy simplistic generalizations. Yes, Americans are the most religious society in the Western world, but they do not accept religion passively. They reframe and reshape religious dogmas. There is a constant dialogue between religion and the contradictory demands of living in a secular, contemporary American society. The sign advertising "coffee, counseling, prayer, and miracles" sums this up so well. It is a recognition of what so many contemporary Americans seem to need—a little physical, emotional, and spiritual "pick-me-up" every day.... And it is an example of how people come up with creative ways to try to meet such needs.

*Anna Bruzzese, Sociologist, Los Angeles Pierce College*

ARGENTINE PEOPLE LIKE TO SAY that the country is all about tango and *fútbol*. And while soccer has remained at the top of national passions, it is only during the last two decades that Argentines (and foreigners, for that matter) have fallen back in love with tango. *Milongas* (as the places in which tango is danced are known) are now everywhere in the city, attracting increasingly younger generations of *porteños* (as the residents of the city of Buenos Aires are known). Nationals and foreigners are seduced by the passion and, at the same time, the melancholia expressed in tango—both in its lyrics and music and, as these pictures wonderfully capture, in the movements of the bodies. Tango is music; tango is dance; tango is also something else, Argentines like to believe. That "something else," the soul of tango, is beautifully portrayed in the light that falls into the two dancers' (or is it lovers'?) performance.

*Javier Auyero, Sociologist, Stony Brook University*

HIDING, BORED, OR HOT? The eye is drawn first to color, second to composition, and only third to wonder about the subjects. But what are they thinking, feeling, expecting?

Three women sit, dressed in bright finery. Two hide their faces behind fans. The third, sitting next to a basket of fresh flowers, looks away and puts her fan between herself and the other two. It's an accidental gesture, perhaps, but there is more distance. On closer inspection, the central figure is blond and relatively pale. On her right is a woman, dark haired but relatively light skinned. On her left, looking bored or a little anxious, is a black woman. The black woman wears bigger jewelry and a bright red wrap in a bow on her head. She has no wedding ring, as the other women do.

And on such seeming details much turns. Are the white women visitors, only for the moment making a matched set with the black woman in the seemingly self-evident unity of the picture? Are the flowers for sale or just bought? Is there an element of play for some where there is work for others? Or have the appearances I have sought to decipher deceived me?

Travel and comparative research alike offer us the chance to project our interpretations onto others they may not fit, but also the chance to break with the illusion that the meanings of the world are obvious. These chances are not options for everyone. Sometimes the world intrudes, sometimes it is sought out. Sometimes interpretation is neither the traveler's play nor the researcher's work but the necessity of someone who lives by sizing up customers to make small sales, or women who must determine whether men are to be greeted with fear or flirtation (or boredom).

Only the woman I guess to be poorer and local puts her bare foot or her face plainly into view. But she is not entirely revealed.

*Craig Calhoun, Sociologist, Social Science Research Council and New York University*

GLOBALIZATION

AMERICAN WAYS OF LIFE have been exported all over the world—even to children, as this photo illustrates. The young Cuban boy has put aside his bicycle for the more sedentary pastime of playing an electronic game. Will the next American export be our obesity epidemic?

*Patricia Pugliani, Sociologist, Stony Brook University*


RACHEL WAS AN EXPERT in showing transitions and unlikely juxtapositions. In many of the pictures, what catches your eye is the unexpected combination of things, the fact that she populates her pictures with inherently unlikely pieces of a puzzle that invite you to put it together for yourself.

Here is a young boy in Cuba, on the doorstep of a building, in what does not look like an affluent neighborhood (cobblestones and raw surfaces), his bicycle leaning against the wall, totally engrossed in a hand-held techno game. The body posture, the way he holds the artifact, and the complete absorption create a familiar picture for all who have children in their lives. Only one doesn't expect it in that neighborhood, in Cuba, and at the end of the twentieth century.

What this picture reminds us of is the extent to which globalization, through formal and informal channels, is covering our world with techno gadgets and the extent to which those gadgets are eagerly, and often unexpectedly, incorporated in people's lives. Here is another example:

Recently we were hiking in the hills behind Chichicastenango, a famous Indian market town in Guatemala that Rachel also photographed. On market days, the town is transformed with vendors coming from the countryside, putting up booths in every street, or just squatting on the sidewalks, especially around the plaza in front of the main church. A wonderful and interesting mixture of Indian and missionary practices carried out side by side. A bedlam of sights and sounds in a cloud of burning copal (incense) on the steps of the main church.

When we'd had enough of the market, we went for a hike in the mountains around the town. We had heard of a stone idol up there, but were rather surprised when we happened upon it. As we prepared to get a closer look, a man and woman arrived whom we took to be a couple. Wrong. Turned out he was a Mayan shaman with his client, an Indian woman in colorful traditional garb. They were preparing a ceremony for whatever problem the woman had.

We ended up standing there for two hours, watching them on their knees, praying with outstretched arms to Pascual Abaj, imploring him to help with whatever was the problem. We watched the shaman build an offering, a circle of sugar, filled with copal, then with dozens of candles of different colors, mostly white and orange, pointing to the center (though the black ones were turned upside down), 12 thick cigars of *tobaco puro,* two cakes of chocolate, candy, and some kind of liquor. At some point he set all of that aflame.

As the shaman was loudly pleading with the spirit, on his knees before the idol, with the woman behind him, arms outstretched, holding bunches of candles—an unbelievable thing happened: the woman's cell phone rang.

She picked it up, talked animatedly for a minute or so (again in *Quiché,* as all of their interaction had been), then handed the phone to the shaman; he talked for another minute, hung up, and they went on imploring the idol without missing a beat. Globalization? Rachel would have loved it!

*Brigitte Jordan, Consulting Corporate Anthropologist, Palo Alto Research Center*

THE USE OF PHOTOGRAPHY AS A QUALITATIVE RESEARCH METHOD continues to increase. In photographs we find stories that teach us about a culture, with hints about history and everyday life contained in a snapshot. A good photograph inspires a researcher to question and observe at the same time. Researchers note and query the photograph's content and its context and the photograph challenges the researcher's beliefs and understandings.

This photograph shows a young boy with a hand-held game. As I have little knowledge of Cuban culture, it makes me raise basic questions about Cuba. The street, the bike, the independence, the mood, the comfort...are these common? What is happening in the day? Is it rare for young children to have hand-held games? The photograph makes me feel uncomfortable with my lack of knowledge of Cuban culture and raises questions I want to answer. That makes for good qualitative research and good sociology.

Photographs can be used as a stand-alone part of qualitative analysis, but more often become part of a larger research agenda. Photography is commonly used early in a research project to help set the stage for what to study and question. If I were to pursue a study of the everyday life of grade school children in Cuba, this photograph would direct me to explore several issues: How do young people use free time? How much free time do they have? What activities, games, toys, and sporting equipment do they have access to? Is there differential access to opportunities for recreation across the culture?

When a photograph can set an agenda for study and provide concrete evidence for answers to questions it is a powerful tool for qualitative researchers.

*Ray Maietta, Sociologist, ResearchTalk, Inc.*

THE BOTTOM OF THE PICTURE shows a corner of a garden with venerable pavilions embodying the ancient Chinese philosophy of "harmony between the human and nature," providing a feeling of peace, indifferent to fame or gain, quiet and gentle.

The center of the photo shows a typical group of modern industrial constructions—factory and chimney; this group prompts viewers to think about the progress and civilization of human beings; but it also suggests that these were achieved through a sacrifice of the natural environment.

The top group of high buildings and large mansions represents postmodern China—urbanization, rapidly increasing population, and the tension between human and natural resources.

In general, the ingeniously arranged view shows the stages of Chinese changing history and puts hundreds or thousands of years of history into one picture. It allows viewers to muse about the development of a society, the movement of human beings, and the relationship between the human and nature.

*Chao Gao, Sociologist, Grandland International*


THE LACK OF APPARENT TENSION BETWEEN THE TWO WAYS OF LIFE, and most likely world views, is remarkable. Both areas look fully functional and active—neither appears on the verge of disintegration nor economically depressed. I was reminded of the debates, both academic and popular, over the word "progress" and thought this photo lent an entirely new meaning to the concept, one that focuses on the coexistence of traditional and contemporary infrastructures and philosophies, cutting across both time and space.

*Staci Newmahr, Sociologist, CUNY, Queens College*


"SUBURB" (*JIAO*) IS A DIRTY WORD IN URBAN CHINA, literally associated with the dirty work of agriculture. Lucky villagers living on the outskirts of cities make a killing offering their property to real estate developers. Increasingly village leaders sell land out from under the villagers, giving them only nominal recompense. This has led to a number of violent social protests in the country. No other country has urbanized so rapidly. As China does so it threatens to erode its agricultural base as rivers, streams, lakes, and air become ever-more polluted.

*Eileen Otis, Sociologist, Stony Brook University*

THE WORLD ON A PLATE: It is striking the extent to which even the simplest foods and beverages testify to a long history of human contact and exchange. In Rachel Tanur's lovely photo, a Guatemalan fruit plate holds a banana (domesticated in Southeast Asia), pineapple (native to South America), papaya (originated in Central America), and melon (originated in Africa; may have been domesticated in Africa, in Asia, or in both).

*Katheryn C. Twiss, Anthropologist, Stony Brook University*

RACHEL'S GUATEMALAN FRUIT PLATE naturally brought to my mind some of our recent research showing that memory manipulation can change what we choose to eat. In research published in the *Proceedings of the National Academy of Sciences* in 2005, we plied research subjects with misinformation about their food histories and induced them to create a detailed story about how strawberry ice cream made them ill as kids. In one study, up to 40% were persuaded that they actually had gotten sick on the ice cream, and now claimed they were less inclined to eat it. In other studies, we have shown that we can plant a positive childhood memory involving a healthy food (asparagus) and people become more inclined to want to eat it. *The New York Times Magazine* published a list of 78 of the "most noteworthy ideas" of 2005. One item that made the list was "The False Memory Diet," based on this research. (The research also made *Discover Magazine*'s 100 top science stories of 2005.)

The False Memory Diet may work by creating or strengthening negative or positive associations to foods. But perhaps there are other ways to accomplish this. Pondering Rachel's Guatemalan fruit plate might be all it takes to make people want to eat more bananas and cantaloupe, rendering The False Memory Diet, as a route to healthier eating, obsolete.

*Elizabeth Loftus, Psychologist, University of California at Irvine*

THE PHOTOGRAPHS TAKEN IN AFRICA profoundly capture globalization's impact on the continent. These images portray the periphery of global capitalism where the signs of local economic backwardness intermingle with those of modern global capital accumulation. We see that local life continues to depend on a shed to house a notary and a bookstore, and revolves around small-scale production of sturdy traditional pottery sold at a local market (P. 101). The notary/bookstore captures the idea of a weak state combined with high rates of illiteracy; one factor contributes to the other, resulting in the absence of local social development. Among these images of poverty and stalled social development, we are no longer surprised to find a ubiquitous sign of globalization—a billboard advertising a stock exchange (P. 113). The billboard is part of another Ghana in the 1990s—where a large-scale privatization program and complete liberalization of international trade paved a way for multinational companies to extract oil as well as to export timber, gold, and diamonds.

*Ania Sher, Sociologist, Stony Brook University*

AFRICA IS A CONTINENT WITH A TREMENDOUS WEALTH OF RESOURCES—timber, oil, and minerals. According to Scott Pegg in "Poverty Reduction or Poverty Exacerbation," Africa is a victim of the "resource curse." Natural resource extraction has not alleviated poverty but rather has fueled its continuance and also exacted severe environmental and social costs in this region. Corruption, authoritarianism, civil war, and government ineffectiveness have also compounded the difficulty of promoting economic growth in the resource-rich countries of Africa. Pegg asserts that resource-rich countries suffer from poor economic growth more than resource-poor countries.

> Between 1987 and 1998, poverty in the region increased by 30 percent. As a result, Africa is now the region with the largest share of people living on less than $1 per day.... According to the World Bank's study, while the sub-Saharan countries contracted by 0.8 percent throughout the 1990s, mining countries in the region did even worse, contracting by 1 percent per year, or 25 percent more than the region as a whole. Perhaps nowhere in the world has resource-led development more spectacularly failed to catalyze economic growth than in Nigeria, where per capita income remains at less than $1 a day, despite the fact that $300 billion in oil rents have been generated over the past 25 years.

Land degradation and population displacement have also been negative side effects of globalization. Natural resource depletion takes the form of air, water, and land pollution. According to Jekwu Ikeme in "Africa and Global Competitiveness: The Neglected Perspective," Western industries incur heavy taxes for degrading the environment. These costs are then factored into the products that they export. Not so in Africa.

> For instance, Food and Agriculture Organization (FAO) reports that the average unit export price of wood products appears to be about 20% less in developing countries than in developed countries. The implication of this is that earnings from these natural asset-degrading productions are often below costs and even if adequate re-investment were to be made, economic loss remains the net result.

Ikeme further argues that multinationals continue to transfer the production end of their businesses to Africa because it costs less than doing business in the highly regulated and taxed developed nations.

> The emissions from such industries pollute the waters of the poor nations causing loss of livelihood for fisherman and farmers, ill health for the general populace, decreasing life expectancy of the citizens of such poor nations, and consequently entailing extra health costs for the poor nations. These health and economic costs are not recognized in the prices of export goods manufactured from such pollution-intensive activities. Conversely, in developed nations, such externalities are captured through adequate taxes and the proceeds used for (i) funding free health care, (ii) research and development in industry-related technologies, (iii) compensation of victims of economic-related pollution, etc. Thus African nations import value-added products from the developed world at relatively environmental cost-embodied prices and sell off their own products at a price less than the true cost.

Although globalization has contributed to the world's progress through knowledge, trade, science, technology, and other cultural influences, it needs reform, especially in places like Africa. To counter the negative effects, Africa also needs to empower itself for the sake of its society. Africa must recognize and develop strategies that harness the potential gains of globalization for its people, and at the same time protect the environment on which its population so clearly depends. Without this reform, poverty and all its associated ills will continue making it very difficult for Africa to compete in the global arena and to shape its own future.

*Elizabeth Boylan, Sociologist*

RACHEL'S PHOTOGRAPH POWERFULLY EVOKES THE ARCH as an architectural symbol of conquest. This massive, brooding archway in Guatemala hearkens to the monumental arches of ancient Rome that celebrate the triumphs of Roman emperors, such as Severus Septimus, Augustus, and Constantine. The Guatemalan arch leads into an imposing Roman Catholic Church—a legacy of Spanish conquest. Christian churches in Guatemala rose on the dust of the Mayan civilization that flourished during the first millennium A.D. The Catholic Church has supported human rights campaigns in Guatemala during the past two decades. However, over the 300 years of Spanish colonialism, churches in Guatemala, as in other Spanish colonies, helped to consolidate Spanish rule. Today, Mestizo (Amerindian and European mixed) populations and Europeans comprise 59.4% of Guatemala's population (2001 Census) and 60% of Guatemalans are primarily Spanish speakers. It is estimated that about 50–60% of Guatemalans are Roman Catholics.

Land seized from indigenous Mayan and other tribes by the Spanish were often turned into coffee, banana, and sugar plantations. The *encomienda* system established by the Spanish forced the Maya and other indigenous people to work on these plantations. Today, Guatemala's poverty is partly rooted in an economy that continues to lean heavily on the export of coffee, bananas, and sugar.

Independence from foreign rule in 1822 brought little relief to Guatemala's poverty-stricken indigenous peoples, since wealth and political power were concentrated in the hands of elites, mostly of Spanish descent. In the 1940s and 1950s, the United Fruit Company—a powerful American company in Guatemala—and the United States government too, conspired successfully with large land-owners and the Guatemalan military to suppress reforms for strengthening workers' rights and distributing land to the poor. In the 1960s, guerrilla movements supported by large numbers of students and peasants rose against Guatemala's military government. The bitter civil war that ensued killed around 200,000 Guatemalans and created over a million refugees. It is estimated that 80% of the victims of murder, torture, and the Guatemalan government's "scorched earth" policies were indigenous people.

In 1996, a peace agreement was signed between President Álvaro Arzú and the guerrillas. The agreement acknowledged that Guatemala's indigenous peoples had been exploited and discriminated against. It was agreed that human rights violations would be investigated and reforms initiated to achieve greater equality. The peace agreement stopped the civil war, but Guatemala continues to face huge challenges in implementing these reforms successfully.

*Niloufer De Silva, Sri Lankan sociologist*

IN CONTEMPLATING CONTEMPORARY GLOBALIZATION the main emphasis should not be placed on looking at the separate "trajectories" of social changes in a particular sphere, but on the interaction between these changes, their interweaving and reciprocity.

The younger generations have accepted this trend of universal changes. Young people live in short time spans ("projects"), without setting themselves long-term goals. An individual evolves as he or she transfers from one "life project" to another. Each "project" (education, a new job, a personal relationship, and so on) blots out the memories of a past "project" in the perception of a young person. Each time, he or she begins everything anew. A significant number of young people are inclined to forget the past and have no wish to stir it up. The retrospective depth of their historical thinking has become greatly reduced. Even the post–World War II era is to a certain extent terra incognita for them. In this context, the new god for young people is not the stability of historical retrospective, not the link between centuries and generations, but a state of constant change. What seems like torment for the older generations is another modus vivendi for the young.

Most young people simply cannot imagine how it is possible to make long-term plans, think about tomorrow, maintain relations with people, and be concerned about one's own authority. For them everything is transient, momentary, and superficial. But this does not mean a decline in morals, rather it is the new reality of globalization. It is bringing with it a new perception of social time, broken down into short "projects" and demands from a person, primarily a young one, maximum mobilization of current resources, and then the rapid transfer to a new project. The world is not likely to return to the old perception of social time. The older generations will have to accept the new concept of time and find their niche in it, not necessarily imitating the youth culture and its style, but by establishing relations with that culture. This constitutes the high art of being beneficial to the younger generation. And this art is a means for maintaining the longevity of the older generations. Any departure into blind defense or alienation is fraught if not with physical, at least with social and psychological self-destruction.

*Nikita Pokrovsky, Sociologist, State University–Higher School of Economics, Moscow*

THE STRIKING CONTRAST between the beauty of nature and the ugliness of human activity—between the seagull and the crane—embodies our growing awareness of the fragility of our ecological system and the need for immediate action aimed at saving the Earth. This awareness has already resulted in various processes in society today. Growing numbers of organizations, such as Greenpeace, institutionalize people's concern, gaining global scale and reach by effectively using mass media and communications to promote their values and ideas. This eco-shift affects the economic and political spheres, resulting, for instance, in numerous international treaties (like the Montreal protocol or biodiversity treaties) that directly influence economic and political processes and dispositions.

*Nikita Kharlamov, Sociologist, State University–Higher School of Economics, Moscow*


GEOLOGISTS BELIEVE that there are 10.4 billion barrels of oil resting beneath the tundra in the Arctic National Wildlife Preserve in Alaska; the high cost of fuel threatens this important animal refuge as oil companies seek access. Environmentalists argue that a web of pipelines and drilling platforms would harm calving caribou, polar bears, and millions of migratory birds that use the coastal plain. Here the seagull seems at peace with the encroachment into the pristine Alaskan wilderness.

*Craig Coelen, Economist; Catherine Haggerty, Survey Methodologist; and*
*John Thompson, Statistician, National Opinion Research Center, University of Chicago*


IN 2000, A STUDY PUBLISHED by a global alliance of conservation groups called BirdLife International found that about 12% of the world's 9,900 bird species are threatened with extinction within the next century. Human activities that cause pollution and habitat loss are primary contributors to the problem, while global warming is an increasing threat. Climate change will likely alter many bird habitats and cause the demise of numerous species.

In 2007 the Intergovernmental Panel on Climate Change consisting of 2,000 scientists from 100 nations concluded that the earth is warming due to the increase of carbon dioxide in the air. However, the demand for the fossil fuels that release this gas when burned and contribute to global warming has not slowed. Pristine environments are degraded through oil exploration and drilling encouraged by powerful fossil fuel industries, government leaders beholden to these corporations, and Americans, who lead the world in consumption.

Although only 4% of the world's population, the United States contributes 25% of the carbon dioxide responsible for global warming.

*Fletcher Winston, Sociologist, Mercer University*


MANY OF RACHEL'S PICTURES ARE SIMPLY ARRESTING, making one pause in wonder. Artists can't control how their work is interpreted. The pictures that most captured my imagination are ones that show people interacting with physical environments, or with environmental possibilities. I look at them and see beautiful scenes, as I'm sure Rachel meant them to be seen. But I also see things that Rachel probably didn't intend her viewers to see. For example, I see Alaska—surely one of the most awesomely beautiful places in the world—with oil in the water.

Serenity and beauty, these pictures show, are part of the human condition. So are their opposites. But we forget that simple truth and thereby increase our vulnerabilities to worst cases. We live longer and better, in rich societies, compared to our ancestors or the poor. This fosters hubris, one aspect of which is a sense of entitlement: that we'll be safe, and that government can keep us safe. Hubris allowed New Orleans to be a city, once. It does the same thing for Los Angeles, Seattle, and Miami.

There are almost 300 million people in the United States and more than half of them live near the seas. Eighty percent of Florida's people live within 20 miles of either the Atlantic or the Gulf of Mexico. Around the world more and more people are moving to the shores, concentrating themselves as if to create targets for hurricanes, tsunamis, earthquakes, and worse.

One reassuring message from disaster research is that people are remarkably resilient, able to bounce back from all kinds of calamities. New York survived 9/11, Alaska survived *Exxon Valdez,* and Florida survived some of the worst hurricanes on record. But we do not know the limits of social resilience because we've not thought deeply enough about how dependent modern people are on their physical infrastructures: What if half of oil production is destroyed? What if all of New York's bridges are blown up? What if a monster hurricane creates a powerful storm surge on Florida's east coast and then travels the short distance across the state to create another on the west coast? What kind of pictures would this scenario generate?

*Lee Clarke, Sociologist, Rutgers University*

THE IRONY OF CULTURAL IMPERIALISM. The clever comment that "You can tell the ideas of a nation by its advertisements" resonates with Americans, and conveys the flavor of self-criticism that characterizes American culture. But its ethnocentrism is reflected in the actual advertisements in the third world. In Ghana, "Own some shares today" (P. 113) becomes an effort to deny the grinding poverty that makes it impossible for 95% of the population to even aspire to such ownership. In Guatemala, the advertisements for Orange Crush and Pepsi Cola (P. 112) reflect the empty calories, imported from America, that contribute to the desperation of an impoverished country.

Only in America do the advertisements reflect "the ideas of a nation." In the Third World the advertisements reflect the ideas of...America.

*Michael Schwartz, Sociologist, Stony Brook University*


AN INTERESTING AND COMPLEX IRONY IS CAPTURED IN THIS PHOTOGRAPH: a message sent not only through the placement of words in a sentence but a metamessage communicated by where the words appear. Advertisements have meaning and "work" because they incorporate and transmit culturally constructed ideas encoded through messages that sell. Had Ben Franklin lived in the advertising age he might have produced this layered aphorism, quintessentially American, celebrating marketing of its own ingenuity as a national product.

The additional complexity here is that the advertising statement appears to be selling the space for an advertisement. The statement itself sends a message to an audience that understands taken-for-granted cultural ideas about creativity, patriotism, and success. But what adds additional complexity is the type of space on which the statement appears—an out-of-use movie theater marquee. For more than a third of the nation's history movie theaters were places for people to go to escape from the worries of everyday life, places where people spent their money and their time. The American experience of the last 25 years has been a process of corporate globalization resulting in a major shift in the mode of subsistence from a manufacturing economy to a postindustrial one. American-based factories have closed and work moved not just out of American cities, but out of the United States. Former "company towns" have become "ghost towns." This advertising for advertisements on the marquee of an abandoned theater sends a metamessage about American experience in the age of globalization.

*Susan Trencher, Anthropologist, George Mason University*

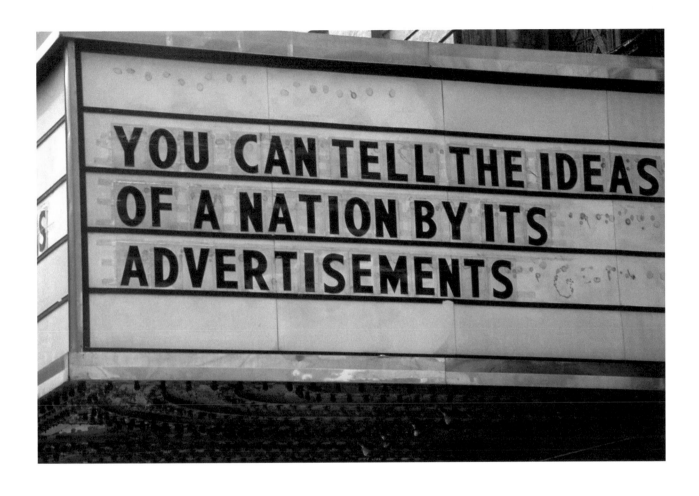

MANY OF THESE PICTURES are both beautiful and thought provoking, but the Ghana stock exchange billboard is irresistible, particularly set next to others: a bookstore advertising all manner of legal services posted on wooden slats (P. 98); mass-produced "traditional" pottery (P. 101); a man and child in traditional (?) costume walking barefoot in the city, grocery carton in hand (P. 71). What's so remarkable about globalization, I think, is not so much its reach as the dependable inconsistency of its effects. These incongruities are not new, but they have intensified in recent decades. Where, one wonders, are that man and child coming from, going to? Who chooses the patterns on that pottery? How many people who can't read and write themselves need to have letters written, to truck in powers of attorney and affidavits, even as the rest of their lives are structured through old or emergent magical beliefs? The pictures don't answer these questions, but they richly raise them.

The stock exchange billboard (P. 113) takes all this to another level, since if anywhere in the rich countries we see an ongoing interaction with magical thinking, it is in the world of stocks and bonds, where individuals are buffeted by forces beyond their control or comprehension. To see that purveyor of new luck and misfortune, standing against the scrubby dirt in Ghana, makes concrete in a way that no words can, the incongruous but nonetheless simultaneous schemas into which globalization has thrown us all.

*Leslie Salzinger, Anthropologist, Boston College*

RACHEL TANUR'S PHOTOGRAPHS represent the true spirit of ethnography. They express a direct, personal, and emotional engagement with the lives of others while also conveying enough intellectual distance to be analytic.

Their play between intimacy and commentary defines the photographer as someone bound to her subject, yet concerned with the larger implications of the images she records. Ms. Tanur understands how something as simple as a street sign (P. 113), a bus (P. 36), or a pile of pottery (P. 101) is an element of an interconnected world in which various social, economic, political, and cultural forces define objects both as just what they are and also so much more.

Ms. Tanur's eye is that of the artist and the social scientist. Her images are beautiful in the tradition of documentary photography. They capture differences in clothing and ritual—whether a Maasai woman's jewelry set against a plaid shawl (P. 57) or multicolored cone hats from a carnival celebration (P. 79). They reflect on widely different architectural styles—the mud walls of an African village (P. 41), colonial homes in Guatemala (P. 50). They provide us with engaging images of markets from around the world (PP. 11–24) and a sense of the profound diversity of distinct cultural practice and their complex links to an ever-more integrated global reality.

For all their detail and informative power, the photos display a fascination with beauty—dark shadows, rich colors, hints of motion and rhythm, and artistry. In this way, these pictures remind us of the woman behind the lens, especially when presented as a collection of years of work and travel.

Ms. Tanur's photos are the record of a life defined by movement, from one place to another across great distances, as well as a spirit of inquiry rooted in empathy. Her images remind us of the expansiveness of our world and the sense in which broad difference can be gathered together. It is to her credit that the many visual ideas she presents hold together as a coherent body of work and that these diverse images are bound to each other by a common ease, comfort, and connectedness between artist and subject.

*Daniel Rothenberg, International Human Rights Law Institute,*
*DePaul University College of Law*

*"I finally reconciled that I am the silent image in my photos —*
*but I am actively there."*

JANUARY 12, 2002

RACHEL DOROTHY TANUR (1958–2002) was not trained as a social scientist, but she cared deeply about people and their lives and was an acute observer of living conditions and interactions. Her profound empathy for others and her commitment to helping those less fortunate than herself accompanied her on her travels and often guided her photography. She delighted in photographing the interaction of people and the artifacts they used and created in such engagements. These, of course, are the raw materials of social science, and Rachel left us a rich legacy of such photos.

Rachel received bachelor's degrees in architecture and city planning from the University of Maryland, a master's degree in urban design from Hunter College, and a law degree from the University of Buffalo. She worked for the New York City Planning Commission for some years as well as in real estate law for several private law firms. She was diagnosed with cancer in 1999. In response, Rachel intensified her pursuit of travel and photography and made several trips to Cuba, South and Central America, Africa, and Europe as well as across the United States before her death at the age of 43.

*Additional photography by Rachel can be viewed at:* http://ms.cc.sunysb.edu/~jtanur *and on the National Science Foundation multimedia website:* http://www.nsf.gov/news/mmg/ *(select Search Multimedia and enter Rachel Tanur).*

WHILE RACHEL HAD HOPED TO HAVE AN EXHIBITION of her photographs during her lifetime, her absorption with living her life as fully as possible kept her from organizing any such show. A year after her death, her family and friends organized a memorial exhibit at Gilda's Club in New York, *Cancer Journeys*. A year later the Social Science Research Council opened its space for another show, *Photographic Journeys*. When Professor Nikita Pokrovsky of State University–Higher School of Economics, Moscow, saw the SSRC exhibit, he was struck by the "human passion and compassion" in the work. He suggested that if the photographs were combined with appropriate commentaries from social scientists articulating their social science implications, the photos would constitute a useful contribution to the field of visual social science. Such commentaries were solicited from social scientists around the world, and, together with some 50 of Rachel's photographs, constituted the 2006 show *Visualizing Social Science* at the National Science Foundation in their Art of Science series. This volume is an extension of that exhibition and part of an ongoing project aimed at encouraging young social scientists to incorporate visual elements in their work.

Commentaries were collected from social scientists after Rachel's death. Hence we often did not know the precise country in which a photo was taken, let alone have any firsthand information about what motivated Rachel to choose a particular subject or to compose a photo in the way we now view it. As a result, there is often ambiguity about the intended meaning of a particular image, in addition to an inherent ambiguity in the interpretation of any photograph or of its contents. Craig Calhoun explicitly refers to that ambiguity in his commentary (P. 88), but it is apparent in many other commentaries as well. Perhaps it is most obvious in the texts referring to the photograph of what we take to be a Chinese family (P. 81), about which the social scientists disagree broadly in their interpretations. Does it document a resurgence of religion in the People's Republic of China or a group of tourists visiting an historical landmark? Are apparent differences in devoutness traceable to gender, to generation, or to party membership? We hope such ambiguities add to the interest of the book rather than detract from it.

Thanks are due to many people who gave generously of their time during the genesis of this project. To Rachel's sister and sister-in-law and to so many of her friends who helped put together the Gilda's Club and the SSRC exhibitions, and to Robert Hite and Nick Wunder who did the technical work for the SSRC show. To Nikita Pokrovsky who first insisted on the social science potential of Rachel's work, and to Cheryl Eavey at the National Science Foundation who undertook to sponsor the show there and Dorothy Harris who made all the essential arrangements. To Paul St. Denis and Eric Yacoub at Stony Brook University who set up the website at which potential contributors could view the photos. To Craig Calhoun at SSRC who saw this as an appropriate project for the Council, and Paul Price who oversaw the editing. To Julie Fry whose own creative spark made the volume the beautiful object it is. To my brother and sister-in-law, Reuben and Arlene Mark, who made possible Rachel's travels to take the photos as well as the publication of the book. And most especially, to the contributors (colleagues, friends, and friends of colleagues and friends) who gave of their aesthetic sensibilities and social science insights to make the commentaries fascinating social science, who responded promptly and good-naturedly to our requests for revisions, and to whom, together with Rachel, belongs the credit for this volume. Quite literally, without their help it would not exist. My heartfelt gratitude, together with that of the rest of Rachel's family, goes to all of these people and to so many others who worked to make this volume possible.

*Judith M. Tanur, Montauk, New York, March 15, 2008*

IMAGE KEY

2

11

13

14

16

17

20

21

23

24

26

29

31

32

33

34

36

36

37

37

39

41

42

45

47

48

49

50

53

57

61

62

65

66

69

71

73

75

76

77

79

81

84

86

124

86

89

91

95

96

98

101

101

102

105

106

109

111

112

113

125

CONTRIBUTORS

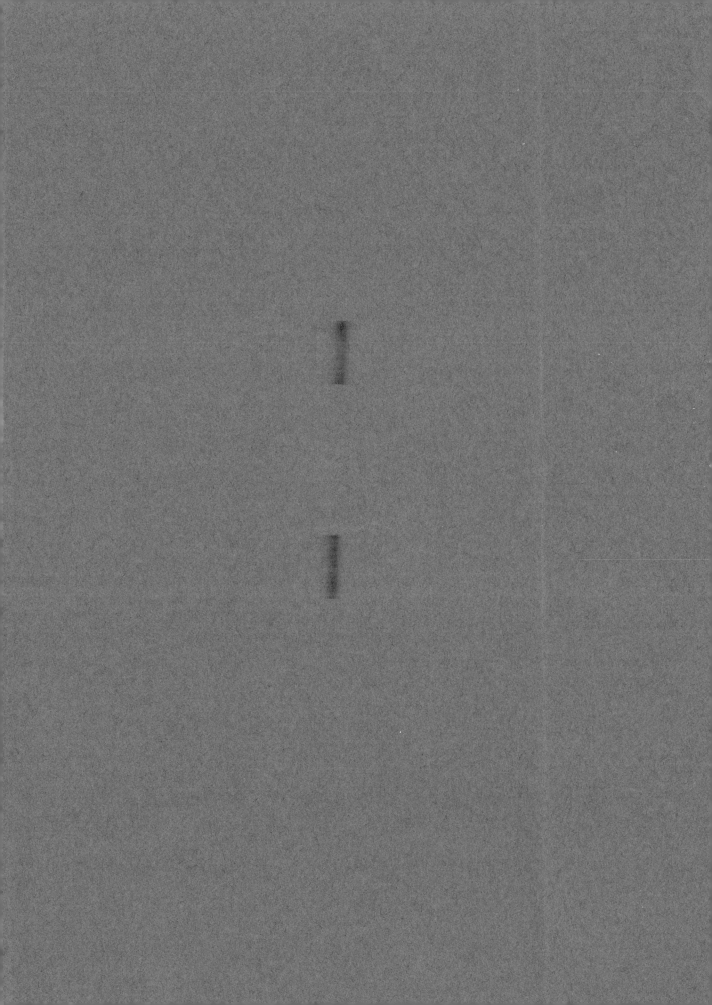